Auto Mechanic's Daughter

Auto Mechanic's Daughter

Karen Harryman

BLACK GOAT
LOS ANGELES

BLACK GOAT is an independent poetry imprint of Akashic Books created and curated by award-winning Nigerian author Chris Abani. Black Goat is committed to publishing well-crafted poetry and will focus on experimental or thematically challenging work. The series aims to create a proportional representation of female, African, and other non-American poets. Series titles include:

Gomer's Song by Kwame Dawes
eel on reef by Uche Nduka

Grateful acknowledgment is made to the editors of the following print and online publications for first publishing these poems or, in some cases, their earlier versions:
Alaska Quarterly Review: "Credo for Odds and Ends"
Connecticut River Review: "Auto Mechanic's Daughter (II)" as "Salvage"
The Cortland Review: "Bourbon Fire"
Dos Passos Review: "Cold War Bride"
Los Angeles Review: "Laundry," "Washing Dishes," "Ventura Burning"
The Newport Review: "Auto Mechanic's Daughter"
Poetry New Zealand: "Confessions"
Her Mark, 2004: "Postcard (II)"
Invisible Plane: "Note to Jesus"
www.inventingtheinvisible.com: "Fishing with My Mother"
www.poetrysuperhighway.com: "White Trash Blessing," "Anne Sexton on Interiors"
www.muse-apprentice-guild.com: "Anniversary," "Newlyweds with Exotic Produce," and "Cold War Bride (II)" as "What Remains"
www.banyanreview.com: "Convalescence"

"Credo for Odds and Ends" was selected for the Syracuse Cultural Workers' *Women Artists Datebook* (forthcoming, 2008).

Published by Akashic Books
©2007 Karen Harryman

ISBN-13: 978-1-933354-36-1
Library of Congress Control Number: 2007926055
First printing

Black Goat
c/o Akashic Books
PO Box 1456
New York, NY 10009
info@akashicbooks.com
www.akashicbooks.com

Acknowledgments

Special thanks to Chris Abani, Ellen Bass, Dorianne Laux, Joe Millar, Frank Gaspar, Cecilia Woloch, Richard Garcia, Eloise Klein Healy, Sarah Gorham, and Jeff Skinner—editors, teachers, mentors, and friends who have helped me begin to find my voice and my way.

Loving thanks to Kirker Butler and to Mary Jacobson, Meghan Adler, Michele Cooper, Katrina Vandenberg, Jennifer Paige, and Ken Fales for graciously reading and rereading these poems and providing conscientious feedback as well as encouragement and support.

Also, thanks to Heath Seymour for meeting and talking with me in Cave City, Kentucky, and for painting *Area 7* for the cover.

And finally, to Johnny Temple and everyone at Akashic Books and the friends, family members, neighbors, and strangers who inspired many of these poems, I am grateful for each of you.

For Barbara, David, and Rachael Harryman

and for Kirker

CONTENTS

III. Blankets and Batteries

IV. Ventura Burning

Introduction

In her debut collection of poems, Karen Harryman has unveiled her myriad gifts as a poet, and they are impressive indeed. Among her considerable talents are her acute powers of observation, her penchant for wedding the gritty with the lovely and tender, her obvious delight in recording small miracles and ordinary pleasures (often rendered extraordinary by her deft eye and mind), her constant celebration of the sounds and textures of language, and her welcome ability to imbue her poems with an emotional freight that creates a lasting pathos. It is this last attribute that so moves me as a reader. For instance, in her poem "Credo for Odds and Ends," Harryman creates a litany of household flotsam and detritus, a list that accrues in a slow and stately manner—adding an (initially) odd emotional tension to the poem—only to surprise the reader with this volta: *"And I will not turn now / windless, to the stars, to God. I will hang my life / on one spare screw."* The revelation that follows these lines (and I will *not* provide it here, thus spoiling the poem's ultimate effect on the reader) is profoundly affecting, evocative, and truly memorable.

This collection contains many remarkable and deeply engaging poems, but my favorite is one that's as *perfect* as any I've ever read during my lifelong love affair with poetry. "Early Evening, Ocean Boulevard" accomplishes a miracle in eight brief lines, merely by painting a visual landscape of the Pacific Ocean that's so accurate and keenly apprehended that it puts the reader in a trance or spell that could be described as a mystical moment outside of time. To achieve such a mental or spiritual alchemy is an incredible poetic feat.

Charting the vicissitudes of her own life, and the travails and triumphs of those whom she knows and loves, Harryman travels great distances in her poems, both internally and geographically, from the Kentucky of her youth to the California of her present (with a detour in Europe). In this movement we encounter moments of wisdom and insight, the small epiphanies derived from love and loss, grief and celebration, dreams and nightmares, curses and blessings, gratitude and despair, and (most importantly) from the daily struggle of living intensely within the *"hours between work and waking / when all you wanted was a piece of the life / you'd dreamed of . . ."*

Maurya Simon
July 2007

I. Limestone and Old Chevys

STARGAZING, DAWSON SPRINGS

For Amy

Here, when the earth passes through a trail of debris,
meteors fall and blaze above brick houses with carports

that lean because someone, a nephew, a sister-in-law,
has backed into the wrought-iron post again. Dinner waits

warm in the foil for fathers driving home from strip mines.
A girl lies on her back on the grassy bank of her parents' yard.

Dew soaks through to her skin as she counts flashes of light.
Sometimes she sleeps during geometry, draws flowers on her knees

through the holes in her jeans. She knows shooting and falling
has nothing to do with being a star, has everything to do with leaving,

lighting up a corner of night along the way. *Someday*, she says,
she'll go far away. She whispers this to her grandmother

who died here, to God, in whom she still believes,
to the night sky, which is big enough to hold her.

EARLY EVENING, OCEAN BOULEVARD

The first time she saw the Pacific Ocean,
out the window of a beat-up Honda,
the sun dropping into the foam-peaked sea,
silhouetted windsurfers' sails and
beached, leafy masses of kelp and weed,
what made her feel like she could stay
were the reverent gulls turned west to watch,
still and quiet as little statues set out in the yard.

COLD WAR BRIDE

Summer, 1949.
Soldiers from Fort Campbell
at ease in groups of four
outside Woodburn's Drugs
laugh *Boy oh boy*
when Edwards tells the one
about the priest
and the hooker again,
slapping their caps
neat as folded letters
against their knees.
Sweat blooms darken
khaki on broad backs,
but stiff creases don't give.
And Naomi's just a girl.
She's not thinking of a husband,
the baby she'll have
next year at 17.
And when she asks
the barrel-chested one
for a nickel, it's for a Coke,
nothing more.

FOR SOME REASON

For some reason
when I see the young mother
underneath the *mercado* sign
pushing a stroller on Alvarado Street
and her older daughter, a dark cloud
sulking behind her,
I think about the time my mother
slapped me hard on the cheek
and I slapped her back.
The girl is 12 or 13.
Her eyes are narrowed
into black-lined slits
and her T-shirt is cut
into a "V"— breasts there
like the pads of curled thumbs.
        I was sitting on the lip
of the claw-foot tub. I remember
imprints of brown and yellow seashells
on the linoleum, the green and white flowers
of the threadbare towel wrapped around her head.
How when my own hand sprang back at her,
I felt like we'd jumped
off a wall together, too high,
like there was no way we'd land in one piece,
no way we'd walk away from this one.
I remember everything,

22

how tired she looked,

the swollen rims of her eyes

already reddening with tears, everything,

except why we had argued,

what I had wanted

that she couldn't give.

NOTE TO JESUS

Sunday nights in church I counted muted panes
of stained glass, scribbled notes on offering envelopes,
ran my thumb over a length of green velvet piping
until it was numb, convinced
my boredom would pierce you again.
When the boy next to me crossed his arms,
I crossed mine. Under the cover of puffy sleeves
we'd ravage palms and pinkies,
imagine our hands caressing lengths
of torso and leg, then pray for forgiveness.
What I know now:
Everything was holy, even Kim, fretful,
her fussy baby working up to full wail in her lap,
her own mother raising an eyebrow from the choir,
and Kim so young, younger than me.
Jesus, I'd do things differently now.
When she carried the squalling bundle
to the vestibule, I'd sneak down from the balcony,
meet her at the back door. We'd leave the babe
with deacons, tear out in a ragtop, a Mustang
on two wheels, rip sleeves and collars from our blouses,
tie shirttails in knots under our tits. We'd dance
to Red Rider in the front seat, let the car drive itself.
Long skirts bunched under one arm, fists
raised to the sunset. We'd circle back
from St. Charles or White Plains

too late for invocation, slip, red-lipped
and flushed like the sky, into that church,
into the back row where we belonged.

AUTO MECHANIC'S DAUGHTER

Evenings after dinner, after dishes,
when she's looking up, searching for a word like *fulcrum*
to describe the night sky resting, with its few bright stars,
on the palm trees in her front yard,
she remembers greasy Saturdays

in the shop on Parker Street,
the bundles of red and blue rags, the pans
of black liquid pushed to the wall, soot clouds rising
from the old sofa worn to the color of flushed midnight.

She remembers nights under ballpark light,
her face fired with sweat and red clay,
her father's hands at rest on the chain-link fence
or cupped to his mouth as he called to her in the field,
the cuts of his knuckles, the moons of grit

under his nails. And earlier years,
winter evenings waiting on the window ledge
of the white-washed Ashland station — red satchel,
a Coke, salty peanuts dropped in one by one.
She barely knew him then, her mother's boyfriend
hunched under the hood of a Ford. At closing time
he took off his cap, loosened his ponytail.

Lifting her to the rusted fender, he said, *Spark plug,*

carburetor, intake valve. He said, *Filter, fluid,*
radiator, hose. He pointed to her heart, said, *Oil*
is the blood. Oil is the blood, like it meant everything.
Pointed to her heart like the world could balance there.

MARA LITTLETON

Mara Littleton lived in a trailer
with her dad's hunting dogs caged
ten feet from her bedroom window.

Evenings she lay in stale-smoke sheets
smelling their urine and feces, nightmaring
herself facedown in the squalor.

Awoke vowing to get out, marry a miner
who hated cigarettes and children, a man
all hers who would plunk it down for a house

with a hot tub, a man strong enough
to pull her back if, straddling him,
she leaned away from the jets, tilted

her head to wet the long, dark hair,
if it caught in the drain, sucked her under.

COLD WAR BRIDE (II)

She was ClingFree and Pall Malls,
breakfast sausage and Aqua Net,
playing cards worn wavy thin from hearts
and solitaire. Pink press-ons skimming
Reader's Digest while laundry spun,
drumming red Formica during *mahjong*
with sisters Bonnie and Amma Jane.
Sometimes, I awake wanting her. My fingers,
stumbling strangers in my kitchen cabinets,
find only Tupperware:
the oil-coated cracker safe,
the lidded cereal keeper.

MY SISTER THE BELLY DANCER

This time when my sister calls
she wants to know what to wear
to her high school reunion. I tell her
it doesn't matter. She's gorgeous,
petite, a belly dancer for Christ's sake.
She was prom queen and homecoming queen,
only one in her ragged class
who lives west of the Mississippi,
but I know what she means. She wants
something to show for the distance.
I forget she got pregnant in college,
didn't come home for months,
that she gave up a daughter,
that she measures every moment of her life
against that severance.
        Damnedest thing, to see her dance,
this little redheaded girl from Kentucky turned
ancient temptress in sequins and veils, glass beads
dripping from her hair, feathers
floating around her hips, tiny rhinestones
on her eyelids, graceful limbs
draped about, and her belly quivering
and undulating like there's something inside her
where the baby was, something else ready to live.

FISHING WITH MY MOTHER

1.

October, the lake holds our stories
and catfish big as cars. Today
the neighbor's recent death, like pollen
on the swollen surface, will not sink.
The soft salesman turned angler
drifts with us all day, our boat
leaning on one pontoon.

2.

Mother knows to twist the hook
ten times before she loops
and tugs the slack with her teeth.
We drift and cast and reel,
lose line, bend hooks. When we speak,
words ride the water like Jesus bugs.

3.

In the wet dark
I've learned the difference
between limestone and old Chevys.
I swim through the windows,
over the hoods. It's a ghost lot
down here, Mother. I am under
deep, a dark fish darting
in and out of the sunken wrecks

settled amongst deer carcasses
long washed clean, bones grown green.
I've made an underwater room:
beanbag chairs and lava lamps,
my first prom dress, and secrets
our baited lines just bump and skim across.

POSTCARD

Black cows by the sea
spectral herd grazing
between bleached fences

and Mary afraid to pee
in the hostel at Pescadero,
remembering quietness
of childhood —
her father asleep
at the end of the hall, the white
underside of forearm rising from
her brother's bedroom doorway,
beckoning, menacing,
portentous as a dead fish.

CONVALESCENCE

The poem I cannot write is rife with Listerine
and oily hairbrushes, horn-rimmed glasses
and dirty pajamas. Makes a dank room
in my brain, slumps amidst tin pots
catching leaks. Invalid with a crooked face
and a wheelchair, the poem is older than me,
will not write itself, so I tend to it daily,
give my life in small bits, eat what it leaves behind.
I don't remember the poem as a young thing,
only this burden having its say, roundabout,
lodged tumor-thick, pressing against my words.

POEM FOR A DEAD MAN'S SISTER

When your brother killed himself,
he left his body half in, half out of the shed
on the deck of his condo, thinking,
as we all do, that the force of a shotgun
would blow him backward.
But he fell forward, onto the wooden boards,
and left a stain, a blood-rimmed
shadow of himself for you
to find along with drafts of notes
he wrote, then threw away.
Not one of the notes, smoothed
and pressed out on his kitchen counter,
told you the truth, which is this:
Long ago, before you were born,
your brother was a good boy,
and the good was ripped from him
by a man he trusted. And where the good was,
the man set down shame and guilt
and covered these with lies. Long ago,
before you were born,
somewhere cold
and dark (before you were born)
over a splintered rail
your brother learned to leave you.

II. The Vista

MALIBU

In May the canyon is poised, brief season
of brilliance and possibility before
summer's hot winds, everything holding,
holding: chaparral, incendiary, stores moxie.
Wild mustard hangs its seeded veil over the path.
Yucca steadies spikes high above the stream
where the newt, circling his mate, rubs his chin to her nose.
Even the toad holds her eggs from cloud-dark water.

This is the time with us, too (maybe you), before
we've been ravaged or before we've been ravaged again.
There's an ocean of luck to the west, no cancer,
no miscarriage, no violent waking to the knock
of highway patrolmen with my husband's wallet,
battered cell phone offered like relics, not today, not now.

KENTUCKY BLASON

Tonight, I'm in love with banjos, bluegrass,
bourbon, with pulled pork shoulder barbecue
(spelled with hyphens, two "Bs," a "Q"), woodpiles,
wood chips, and old-timey wood-burning stoves,
but also blue-hairs with horse money,
sorority girls buying quilted bags
at Jacobson's in the Mall St. Matthews.
And Old Louisville, 4th Street, my apartment
across from Winn Dixie, the dumpster where
they found the dead man. I'm in love with black-top
highways 109, 62, and 31-E,
drive-thru liquor stores, Dad's old pickup,
the red Ford before the blue Chevy,
before the gray Toyota, but also the blue Chevy,
and cousins doing time for running meth labs
in bathrooms. I miss aluminum siding and porches
with junk piled just high enough to set your coffee cup.
I miss chili suppers and raffles and bingo.
Tonight, even church, even rednecks. Say
you love me, too, Kentucky. Say we belong
together. Smoke a cigarette and say
you forgive me for losing my accent,
making cornbread with a mix, and paying too much
for blue jeans, rent, and shampoo. Forgive me
for laughing when you're the punch line.
Say "Fiddlesticks." Call me "Sugar." Say I can come back
anytime; nothing has changed, I'm still your girl.

MORNING IN BURBANK

After Mary Oliver

It starts like this:
Sun crowns the sweat-spangled
forehead of a bald neighbor
swinging his arm weights
past Warner Brothers, Gate 11,
under the wet arc of sprinklers.
And always the poet, risen
earlier than the screenwriter in her bed
and the comedian on her sofa,
is smug, having seen him first,
believing this business
of birds and worms.

ANOTHER YEAR

To stick it out another year was to know
the agent would come around,
the studios would hire.
It was to believe in yourself, foresee
the big check, the parking space,
your name painted there.
   Jogging again, on New Year's Day,
past the house that smells of piss
and wet leaves, to stick it out
another year was to accept the plastic
hair clip you lost last summer
(now shattered, half-ground
into the concrete) as an artifact
instead of an omen.

ANNE SEXTON ON INTERIORS

She was all money, crisp and green,
folded discreetly in an old gold clip.
I remember the fabric shop,
the way she leafed
through the bound samples
of thick brocade florals.
Then, the book on the floor,
lifted her heel,
removed the white sandal, and stroked
a swatch of velvet with her long toes
like it was Tuesday
and she, home alone, was just
climbing the walls, just
walking on the furniture.

LEPIDOPHILE

Erotic little Golden Guide
of St. Martin's Press

your pages flutter and tease
like the butterflies you list.

How *do* we keep our clothes on
mouthing *alfalfa looper* and *rosy maple,*

and who was that horny lepidopterist
who named the *spicebush swallowtail?*

WASHING DISHES

The man washes. The woman dries. She wanders off, combs her hair, stares at her pores in the mirror, waits for him to fill the rack, comes back. I dreamed we had this baby, he says, leaning on the sink. We were at this party, there was a pool, he says. I didn't want the baby to go near the pool, but the baby jumped in or fell and I went in after it, of course, but there was dirt in there and leaves, and—get this, he says, something shiny caught my eye. I swam to it, he says. That's it, that's the story. That's why I can never be a father.

You wouldn't do that. You wouldn't forget about the baby, she says, and slips her wedding band from the souvenir holder on the sill. It is a silent argument they have, she studying his lips, his brow, conjuring a child with his features. He, doubtful, terrified, chasing spoons and cereal bowls through murky water.

LAUNDRY

Just after takeoff
she looks out at the lights,
the tip of the wing.
If part of it peeled back,
spiraled down,
and she was the only one to see,
she would pull the tiny shade.
She would touch his forearm,
mouth, *I love you.*
He would remove his headphones,
say, *What?* Maybe, *You're pretty.*
And it's enough.
Just like when he's watching TV
and she brings the laundry
warm from the dryer.
He pats the cushion beside him.
She pours it out for him to fold.

NEWLYWEDS WITH EXOTIC PRODUCE

After a fight, I send him alone to the store
with a list of foods he's never heard of, like mesclun
and lychee, tahini, plum tomatoes and tarragon.
In that hour I decide I can live without him, poor, lonely,
But there are cats, I think. I could go back to my parents on the lake,
convert their shed, write poems about loons and fish; cats.
I tell him all this when he returns buckling
with full sacks of groceries. I am crying, choking.

Slowly, carefully, he says, *It's "lee-chee," not "lie-chee."*
The produce man helped him, sliced one open for him in the aisle.
In our kitchen, he pulls one from the bag, tears the thick paper skin,
cuts through to something hard with his knife, says
(coaxing the pulp, holding it inches from my mouth),
This is the part you eat.

THE VISTA

In our new neighborhood
we have one of those restored movie houses
that shows first-run movies, the best
of the past and the present, digital sound,
great popcorn and rows spaced wide enough
to drive a golf cart through.
The red velvet seats, the baroque likenesses
of pharaohs and goddesses under-lit
by geometric sconces —
it's so beautiful Kirk doesn't bristle
when the stranger's kids in the front row
become restless, run up and down the aisles,
chase each other through the rows.
When the lights dim, he grips my knee,
a twinkly-eyed boy again, remembering
the first time he saw a light saber.
We've been together six years.
Every day is better than the last.
Outside, underneath the marquee,
Sunset Boulevard is all neon and streetlights.
There is a blue bicycle chained to a rack.
It has pinstriped fenders,
a white wicker basket with plastic flowers.
I want to touch it. I want to touch everything
to know it's real.

MAGNOLIA BOULEVARD

Where you go if you need pistons or tile, stereo speakers for your car. Home of Frenchy's Beauty Salon, Barstools Unlimited, not far from Chili John's. Jugular vein of the Valley. Cut it, it bleeds Valvoline and clots of rubber stamps. Two miles south of here on monochromatic lots, in soundstages that look like factories, young men and women with lattés and lunch dates are going to work in expensive shoes and dirty denim, making TV with all the gusto of children grinding bright Play-Doh through holes in plastic, calling it spaghetti, seeing who'll bite. And even when the country has her face over the bowl, salty noodles hanging from her chin, parents will worry about long-term security, voice concerns at Christmas and Chanukah. We are all like Henrietta who simply loved her schnauzer. Thirty years ago when she left the secretarial pool to set up shop, groom dogs for a living, it seemed frivolous, a little silly to her father, a little scary to her mother. And it's no different for you, alone at a desk you've turned toward a window, with your stories and poems, your paintings or songs in your head. Each night, someone who loves you prays that you're safe, prays that you fail.

ANNIVERSARY

Years ago, driving to California, road heat rising
through metal, black can of a car, we dipped
our toes and wedding towels in the cooler,
began each day moving forward, covering ground.
At night we rested, swaddled in the sting of Motel 6 sheets.

Mornings after nights when doors slam, keys skid,
and grocery bags split on impact, I rise early, listen
to the lawn dry, witness your slow, tremulous waking.
Our marriage ticks off with the sprinklers. Heat-
forged and simple, we begin again and again.

III. Blankets and Batteries

DREAM IN WHICH MY MOTHER HAS FALLEN ASLEEP IN THE BATHTUB

In the dream in which my mother has fallen asleep in the bathtub, I know something is wrong before I walk in on her body already floating to the surface, but I am strong and she is no more than a wet towel folded over my arms. I wring water from her lungs and beat life back into her with my fists. She gives her head a wet dog kind of shake and says something like, *Well, that was a close one.* Then, *Who's ready for chicken à la king?* We chop carrots. I remember there was a knife when she said (and this is the strange part), *Before I had you, I dreamed that I cut off my hand and gave it to a little girl.* Now, I do not know much about dream interpretation, but to me that says when a baby comes, there are some pretty obvious sacrifices. And I'm about to ask her what she gave up, when just like that, just like she's reading my mind, she says, *Don't worry so much*, and tosses me a package of frozen chicken, which, now that I think about it, was probably a bunch of hands.

LOW COUNTRY BOIL

Blame the blue sage, spicy, on the trail
our morning hike in Wildwood Canyon
that first spring in California. Say it drove us
to sausage, shrimp, and corn out of season;
that we laid newspapers,
set amber lights before our friends' faces,
layered a speckled pot with new potatoes
because we were grateful for the March rain
that let the stream run to the moss-green rock
of the reservoir, reminding us of home.
Say it was share some blessed thing or burst
from gratitude for new friends, a house,
and this thick table of red oak.
Or say blessings come because we let them
and think of a Sunday in Kentucky
when you said, *California?* and I said, *Why not.*

SUNNY PINES

Of the trailer park in Jacksonville Beach
I remember sifting through my toy box,
the tinder of hand-me-down things:
busted teacups, dolls, their plastic hands
tattooed with marks broken crayons leave.
Sand in carpet, the bathtub, on linoleum
beneath the tough pads of my bare feet.
The sepia dusk, yellow porch lights pulling
workers home from the paper factory,
Mom in her steakhouse apron and skirt,
animal mother nudging me up the crumbling steps.

ODE FOR A TORNADO

Cavalier weathermen say we're due an earthquake.
We could be anywhere when a big one hits, alone
in cars under overpasses, the dentist, the mall.
I prefer tornadoes, the civility of warnings,
Rhett Butler riding up on a blond horse
telling us we need to be kissed.
All that time for gathering matches
and candles, crouching by the radio
in the basement, the good, wet dark of childhood,
worms churning black earth of crawl spaces
behind little doors, knowing something's out there
just ahead, big and dangerous.
I want the tornado of '75,
the house on Cedar Street, our basement,
foam-green paint, cracked,
curling up concrete walls,
my mother singing "Landslide"
to the guitar my father remembered
along with blankets and batteries,
the percussion of screen doors losing grip
overhead, sideways sheets of rain,
the wind and leaves, the three of us
backed up against shelves of Mason jars
humming in their rusty lids,
all that delicate fruit preserved and quivering.

TODAY THE POEM

Today the poem is wound in sour laundry left too long in the
bottom of the hamper. It is the wood grain shining beneath lay-
ers of dust and dog hair, forgotten product of elbow grease and
tears; somewhere unattainable, there's another poem. About
Kentucky? The truck driver's face. Or the hard little girl behind
the counter. I am not doing this right. We're at the Kwik Stop
in Burkesville. My grandmother looks wild-eyed, lost, asking
strangers if they know my cousin, saying his name over and
over again into her new cell phone. I'm watching her from one
of those Formica booths where you can sip a Coke, collect your
thoughts, consult a map, or maybe pile up the scraps of your
life in notebooks, thinking someday you'll do something with it;
someday, someone will care that you were here, that you tried to
be good, that your mother worked hard to raise you but couldn't
really protect you. From what, you'd rather not say, because af-
ter all this has become a poem about death, his slow and constant
circling of our block, perverted mumble from his beat-up car,
asking something of us always, who we'd miss, if we're happy, if
we'd like a ride.

BOURBON FIRE

Every few years, lightning found a wooden storehouse
of one distillery or another in that green pocket of Kentucky
where the world's whiskey is made,
where I learned to swirl bourbon in a glass,
taste a coffee finish, learned to tell time
by the smell of sour mash in the air.

Heaven Hill burned for days.
We'd watch from the grocery store parking lot
for spikes of flame through smoke, never close enough
to see what the volunteers described, the barrels full, aflame,
blown-out stories of gray timber cascading down to the river,
the catfish and bluegill straining to breathe
beneath the bourbon slick.

I've forgotten everything else,
spent most evenings with a girl named Bobbie
draining beers, shooting pool, throwing darts,
flirting with truck drivers and college boys,
driving home with the top down, long scarves wrapped around
our heads,

iced Maker's & Cokes sweating between our thighs.
We were ablaze as you might have been, hours between work
and waking
when all you wanted was a piece of the life you'd dreamed of

or all but ruined—what you had coming

because you were good,

because you were beautiful, spilling all you knew.

RITUAL

Sundays, after I quit the church, Kerri and I
would sleep until noon in the dorm, wake to spears
of sunlight stabbing through slatted window blinds.
Tongues thick from beer and cigarettes, smoke
married to our hair, last night's eyeliner
a sullen sunset across puffy cheeks. In soft focus
she'd step over our clothes, pad down
to the ice machine with plastic cups clean enough
for Diet Coke. Over cold lo mein
or pizza from a box on the floor, we'd pull
the stories from Saturday's haze. I could never
hold my liquor, was always fighting
with our roommate or cheating on my boyfriend.
Chin propped on one elbow, she'd take my confession,
forgive me for the week's transgressions, and
ceremoniously bring out the jar, St. Ives
Mineral Clay. She'd sink her fingers deep
into mint-green mud the color of church walls,
the scent of old hymnals. She'd tip my face back,
she'd smooth it over every pore.

CONFESSION

You see your friend,
her graceful shoulder now turned
with purpose from the bar
toward a stubby insurance broker
raising his glass.
Working girls glide on lip gloss,
flavoring highballs slick coconut
and petroleum cherry.
Nothing about this is easy,
and you've bothered
to wear uncomfortable shoes.
You'll bow out long before last call,
long before the broker's number is tucked
inside a spectrum of lacy bras
and they've all got plans for Mexico.
What you want is someone else's pain,
to taste it, suck it from the bone.
You want your friend to fall
through your door at 4 a.m.,
and speak, eyes closed,
of how she's never felt so alone.

LEXINGTON

Those days, in my sublet apartment,
the owner's wiry hair lay in gray drifts

in the corners of the bathroom, awaiting
his return. Mornings, the October light

tested the seams of black basket clouds,
and I could never firmly grasp the dew-slicked

handle of my borrowed Buick, always chipping
a nail or two. Wet newspapers sweated

and crawled from their plastic, spackling
themselves to the carport week after week.

It was my first job. I was teaching
A Separate Peace and fucking it up.

WHAT MATTERS NOW

The last steel beam carried away today.
Bodies now fine as sifted flour,
and men and women have searched with buckets
and garden rakes. How many fingers. How many toes.
How many bruises. How many truckloads
of bone-dusted memorandums. Bulldozers,
backhoes, man hours (the occasional

clump of dirt stuck in my shoe, a thumb sliced,
a paring knife). Multiply.
And multiply. I do not think of shoe bombs,
airport security. I resist the thought of lawyers
and tax ID numbers. And I do not think
this poem matters, except to say
I think about your finger,

how I would hope to know it,
pick it from a pile if I had to. Tonight,
by the moon, I'll catalog your parts,
each hair, every fold and swell.
I'll hold your pink hand to my lips
and whisper goodbye.

CREDO FOR ODDS AND ENDS

I believe in the good pen bleeding black
across scraps of paper, backs of envelopes,
receipts, half-spent notebooks, cardboard
covers long ripped from spiral wire.
I believe in thick coffee tables and crumbs
from last night's dinner, rings from glasses
of once-cool water. I believe in the house
that is never clean, in quilt scraps and bits
of yarn, ravelings and threads. I believe in piles
and crooked stacks and palm fronds that drop
without warning to litter the lawn.
In batteries and bulbs, hard evidence
of the junk drawer, the knot of forgotten wire,
loose leaves of gum. And I will not turn now,
windless, to the stars, to God. I will hang my life
on one spare screw. Who does not want,
does not need a broken lock, a frayed oven mitt
to turn over and over—tenuous, precious, useful.
Let me start again. A little girl has died:
A father touches one yellow sock to his lips.

CANCER SUNDAY

Day of Naugahyde chairs and orange
sherbet day of flavored mouth swabs
day of perox-a-mint and other hyphenated
products you imagine the suct-o-lung
evac-u-gel this is the day of nurses with lisps
in happy-face scrubs the undertow
of a cough the hankie marbled with blood
the pink plastic spittoon day
of snack food and jangling change
in the preacher's pocket day of prayer
and pimento cheese sandwiches day
of ice soup strawfuls dripping
slowly down the dry tongue
the long low fluorescent bulb and string
on this the day of Vaseline and whispering
against his rattling breath
this is the day he works with his fists
under hard white sheets until death
is smooth-edged and useful
a thing you can hold.

MARY, GRIEVING

1.

She shuffles room to room
concave from slumping graveside
in the dirt. Facedown on her bed
she's limp as muslin
draped over an empty bowl.

2.

Lunchtime, she calls crying again.
Phone wedged between shoulder
and chin, I scrape bits of hard-boiled
egg into a dish, say, *Turkey, bread,*
cheese. Sit, breathe, eat.

3.

Sometimes I draw inward as if
on a crowded elevator, as if her grief
was a cluster of stale molecules
rising up from a stranger's coat.

4.

Instead of talking, we run errands,
the library, the grocery store.
When I stop the car to let her out,
I know she wants to die.
Her girl's been gone six months.

Life is reeling past us both.
Milk is warming in the trunk.
Outside the window, monarchs
big as birds again
tumble over the hedge.

IV. Ventura Burning

POSTCARD (II)

Just the wood-grained
counter of this diner
that serves olallieberry
pie on white plates

and my friend small as a child
in her hat, unemployed, alone,
who tells me she wants to paint
the berry-smeared plate,
the sliver of moon caught
in craggy silhouettes
next to the lighthouse, anything
that's right in the world.

AT LEAST

In May and June
there are the jacarandas'
purple blossoms fallen
on green lawns of every block

reminding me of home
how bluegrass isn't blue
until it gives up that flower
until it goes to seed.

UNE PETITE RÉSISTANCE

A professor in a life vest stamped *Collette* divided the last of the millet on the heavy wooden table. We are French and polemic, a knot of bedraggled artists and unlikely literati hunkered down, dirty strips of once-white sheets for doors. It's a Peter Sellers movie dream, the enemy coming first in planes far overhead, then popping up in glassless windows. Once, they tipped the shack like a snow globe, and Louis, François, and I rolled toward the wood-burning stove. I shoved Robert (my cousin who normally paints rabid wildcats on motorcycle jackets) under the bed until they came for us. The enemy was a beautiful woman, black jacket tied at the waist, sleek leather boots, and a straight nose. *Make me long for something,* she said, smoothing her dark ponytail. *Make me want something.*

Robert crawled out and we pulled three mismatched chairs up around the stove. I told her all I knew, what I learned from my father who grew up on an Army sergeant's pay, the oldest of seven brothers and sisters. *First, want what you have.* And Robert, who's 34 and disabled from a back injury he got lifting the tire of a semi-truck, Robert, who lives in constant pain, said through the gaps of his missing teeth, *Yeah, want what you have, then it don't hurt to dream.*

WHITE TRASH BLESSING

May we rise up from nicknames
and schoolyard taunts. Rise up
from harelip legacy, burred heads
and matted braids liceless
against the wind. May the dogs
in plywood pens eat beef tonight
and root, unscolded, the banks of creeping phlox.
May the mines, the factories, the diners hire.
Checks, may they always come in.
Let broken toys regenerate
in grassless yards. Handlebars
will sprout tires, frame, banana seat.
On playgrounds, secondhand pant legs
and sleeves will trail and flap in extravagant folds,
releasing clouds of shame into a coal-town breeze,
and our names won't rhyme with anything.

PORTLAND

Here, the red pear dissolves
on the tongue. The bread
is warm and dense;
the coffee, thick, black.
Everything else, even sunlight,
unsettling, white.

MALLORCA

Today, a field of mustard
and slick green shutters, crooked
on the house of rocks.
Roof tiles glittering dully
like beans or macaroni
glued to a cigar box,
one I would make for you,
hold to your ear
so you could hear
the bleating of goats
lost in a buzzing thicket,
the dumb clink
of their bells.

MALLORCA (II)

Port de Pollença midmorning
and the sea is a child's drawing
with sailboats, the sun in the corner,
and scalloped blue lines, waves,
cutting wet crests into the sky
which is white
behind the black "M"s of seabirds.

And on the beach, I am sticks
and circles in a block of green shirt,
a tilted triangle of windblown skirt;
my arm, a capital "L" waving out to you.

THE TRUTH

Monday morning rush hour on the tube, our second day in London,
Kirk is wearing a windbreaker and a red baseball cap
which stands out against the pinstripes and powdery swathes
of wide-knotted silk ties,
stands out against elegant pashminas looped
and tucked inside tailored overcoats.
One hand in the pocket of his Levi's,
the other grasping the yellow rail above his head,
hips pitched forward in a cat tilt, shoulders slumping a little
under the weight of his backpack.
I look down at my book,
read the same paragraph for three stops.
Might as well have married that country lawyer's son,
drive an SUV to church on Sundays, make casseroles
with cans of mushroom soup and bags of Tater Tots.
Might as well fake orgasms and give money to Republicans
because on this train, scritching along its mated track
hundreds of feet below London's quaintly cobbled streets,
my husband's awkward as a scuba diver.
Full wet suit and clumsy gear, rubber flippers in everyone's way,
oxygen tank clanking Morse code
against the metal wall of the coach, his message:
I have money to burn,
and you're all a bunch of working stiffs.

And by now, maybe you're expecting me to soften, turn

to redeem him. I could implicate myself, offer a realization
in metaphor like creamed tea and frosted cakes you could nibble
or politely decline. I could paint him saintly, bending
to lift the stroller for the pregnant woman, giving his seat.
Or spiritually, pressing his forehead against a standing stone at
Avebury; then,
sweetly, plucking a dandelion from the ancient grass, tucking it
inside my journal, but I won't do it. That's not what happened
anyway.
The truth is we stepped off the train together
and went on loving what it is that we don't hate.

MOON WITH A RING

Driving home after a movie
we cannot name the silence
between us. The moon is doing that thing,
disappearing and reappearing
in other windows through holes
in the dark clouds,
like it has something to say.
I'm 14 again, dreaming and needy.
I want you to swerve to the curb,
kiss me, pull me from my seat onto a dirt path
in some afterthought of a park
between apartment buildings. Vow
there, beneath high-tension wires,
that you will not die before me, you will never
leave me for the blond production assistant
with the math degree. I want you to say it.

      In seconds, we are home. It is late,
the street, quiet. Our neighbor
sits alone at a blue table
under fluorescent kitchen light.
She has her head in her hands again.
Her husband died last September.
A full moon of white hair,
a ring of throbbing hands.

STAG BEETLE

Sleek black worry stone with legs,
she lives beneath decaying logs,
dines on honeydew and sap oozing
from decaying leaves and bark.
Her eggs, whitish larvae, hatch and sip
sweet juices of rotting oak,
willow, apple, and cherry trees.
She, too, is most vulnerable at home,
easily collected at night flying close
to the nest. Makes this buzzing sound,
little prayer. Gratitude gives her away.

POSTCARD (III)

Not the golden hour's long shadows
over vineyards, their gilded names,
Mondavi, Rombauer. Not the cellars,
dark honeycombs of ripening wine.

But the busboy, bored with sunsets at 14,
who, propping a leg on the low stone wall,
brushing a tuft of sage with his hand,
knows no better than to ask why I'm alone,
his stippled chin close enough to hold
in both my hands when he says,
Write something about me.

CUSTODIAN IN WINTER

The parking lot is empty.
Almost-snow swirls above pavement,
settles on tree roots
like chalk dust on chapped hands
that wipe slate day after day,
sweep paper from tile.

VENTURA BURNING

Open and nervy, I find work for myself.
I am fire keeper. All weekend I seek

dry grass that ignites, does not smoke,
feeds instead of smothers. We buy wood

because what we found was wet
and slight. I pile paper, break twigs, sticks,

drag branches to the pit, crack them with my heel.
At night I sleep moments broken by nightmares:

The salesman and his wife beside us are vagrants
pissing on our tent, stealing our keys, purses.

Sister and friend are oblivious. Everything,
the mustard blooming beside the freeway,

the Amtrak line behind our site,
the Pacific Ocean, my husband, too,

is new and good. There's time to turn inside,
to think, *Fire*. Stir embers, coax hot ghosts,

layer wood, arrange for air, breathe, predict
what will fall first, next, to the coals.

AUTO MECHANIC'S DAUGHTER (II)

In Los Angeles, I look to the river
stanched by a lawn chair and a few dead leaves

to know I belong. With sticky thighs,
gutful of sloe gin sloshing, I've stumbled up

from greener banks to discover the use of broken things
misplaced, the three-legged sofa in the forest. I know

where debris collects, in fencerows and tufts
of tall grass, how it hovers over the tracks

long after the train, the stained glass
of red cellophane caught in chain-link.

Forget that the hills are sliding down,
that they sometimes burn—fiery, teetering

chrysanthemums pinned tenuously to the night.
Forget the 50-foot yacht slid from its trailer,

blocking rush-hour lanes, composing
this city's surrealist foreground. Forget

the studio exec careening in his convertible.
To make it here, I live for what I know,

the busted doors of this furniture truck carting cushions,
bundles of down, for the oblivious truck driver driving

and singing, for the wake of white feathers
spilling out, blowing up from my wheels like snow.

Other selections in Chris Abani's Black Goat poetry series

GOMER'S SONG poems by Kwame Dawes
72 pages, trade paperback original, $14.95

Gomer's Song is a contemporary reinterpretation of a Bible story. Gomer, a harlot, was the wife of the Old Testament prophet Hosea. But even after marriage to Hosea, she refused to conform to her expected role. In Gomer, poet Dawes finds the subject for a beautiful contemporary exploration on the cost of arriving at freedom with an uneasy grace. This is tender a book with profound lyrical insights.

EEL ON REEF poems by Uche Nduka
152 pages, trade paperback original, $15.95

Award-winning Uche Nduka challenges every expectation of an African poet. His unique voice is a heady amalgam of Christopher Okibo, A.R. Ammons, John Ashbery, Kamau Brathwaite, and something only Uche can bring. In reading Nduka's poetry, the reader is encouraged to enjoy each instant, each image, while resisting the instinct to construct linear meaning in the poems.

Also Available from Akashic Books

SONG FOR NIGHT by Chris Abani
164 pages, trade paperback original, $12.95

"Chris Abani might be the most courageous writer working right now. There is no subject matter he finds daunting, no challenge he fears. Aside from that, he's stunningly prolific and writes like an angel. If you want to get at the molten heart of contemporary fiction, Abani is the starting point."
—**Dave Eggers,** author of *What Is the What*

"Not since Jerzy Kosinski's *The Painted Bird* or Agota Kristof's Notebook Trilogy has there been such a harrowing novel about what it's like to be a young person in a war. That Chris Abani is able to find humanity, mercy, and even, yes, forgiveness, amid such devastation is something of a miracle."
—**Rebecca Brown,** author of *The End of Youth*

BECOMING ABIGAIL by Chris Abani
A selection of the *Essence Magazine* Book Club and Black Expressions Book Club
128 pages, trade paperback original, $11.95

"Abani is a fiction writer of mature and bounteous gifts . . . Abani, himself incarcerated and tortured for his writings and activism in Nigeria in the mid-'80s, writes about the body's capacity for both ecstasy and pain with an honesty and precision rarely encountered in recent fiction . . ."
—***New York Times Book Review*** (Editors' Choice)